The Monsters Project Book

CONTENTS

Nessie - the most famous monster in the world! • • • • 2

More lake monsters • • • • 4

Monsters of the sea • • • • 6

Underwater people • • • • 8

Mountain monsters • • • • 10

More mountain monsters • • • • 12

Real monsters? • • • • 14

Mythical monsters of Ancient Greece and Rome • • • • 16

More mythical monsters • • • • 18

Gigantic trouble! • • • • 19

Dragons! • • • • 20

Transformation monsters! • • • • 22

Monster-spotting • • • • 24

Man-made monsters • • • • 26

Science fiction and fantasy monsters • • • • 28

A monster map • • • • 30

Index and acknowledgements • • • • 32

STEVE SKIDMORE • STEVE BARLOW
Illustrated by Andrew Warrington

BROCKHAMPTON PRESS
LONDON

Nessie – the most famous monster in the world!

LOCH NESS IS:
- *THE LARGEST FRESHWATER LAKE IN THE BRITISH ISLES;*
- *38 KM LONG (24 MILES);*
- *2.5 KM WIDE AT ITS WIDEST POINT (1.5 MILES);*
- *OVER 250 METRES DEEP.*

Most people have heard of Nessie, the Loch Ness monster. The monster is supposed to live in the cold, peaty depths of Loch Ness in Scotland. Nessie is probably the most hunted monster in the world, but, despite all efforts, no one has captured a clear photograph of her, him or it!

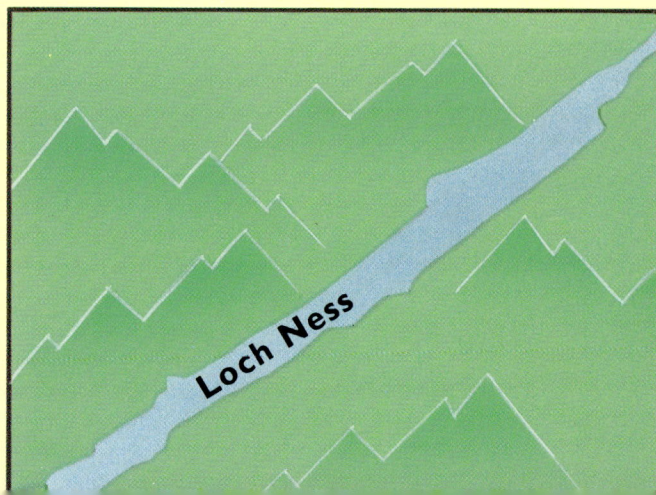

Loch Ness is connected to the sea by a series of other lochs. There have been reported sightings of a monster in Loch Morar. This monster has been nicknamed Morag. But could Nessie and Morag be one and the same or do they belong to a family of monsters?

The first sighting of the monster

In the year 565 AD, St Columba, on his way to visit a Scottish king, stopped at Loch Ness. According to legend, one of the saint's followers began to swim to the other side of the Loch to get a ferry coble (rope). Whilst swimming across, the man was attacked by a

Loch Ness

water monster. St Columbus saw this and drove the monster away by calling on God and saying, 'Thou shalt go no further nor touch the man; go back with all speed.'

Modern sightings of Nessie

It wasn't until the twentieth century that interest in Nessie began to grow. The first modern sighting occurred on 14 April 1933. Mr and Mrs John Mackay were driving home when they saw an enormous animal in the water. They told their friend, Alec Campbell, describing the animal as being about six feet long and having a long, tapering neck, a smallish head and a huge hump. From this time on, Nessie captured the imagination of the world and thousands of sightings have been reported. Today scientists are using more and more sophisticated methods in order to gain evidence of Nessie's existence.

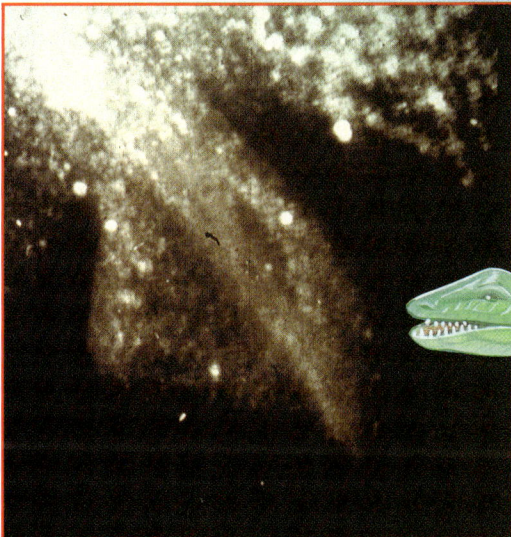

These underwater photographs were taken by a remote control camera. Some experts claim that they show part of a flipper. This has led to some people claiming that Nessie is a prehistoric creature, a member of the **Plesiosaur** family.

Amazing FACTS

NESSIE HAS BEEN GIVEN AN OFFICIAL SCIENTIFIC NAME BY THE NATURALIST SIR PETER SCOTT. IT IS CALLED NESSITERAS RHOMBOPTERYX.
BUT IF YOU REARRANGE THE LETTERS, YOU GET THE MESSAGE: MONSTER HOAX BY SIR PETER S!

More lake monsters

Nessie is not the only lake monster in the world. There have been thousands of reported sightings of lake-living monsters from all over the world. However, there is still no definite evidence that such creatures exist.

Ogopogo

Many of the lakes in North America have monster stories or legends attached to them. Probably the most famous North American lake monster is **Ogopogo.**

Ogopogo is supposed to live in the water of Lake Okanagan in British Columbia, Canada. The lake is wider and longer than Loch Ness, and the history of the monster goes back hundreds of years.

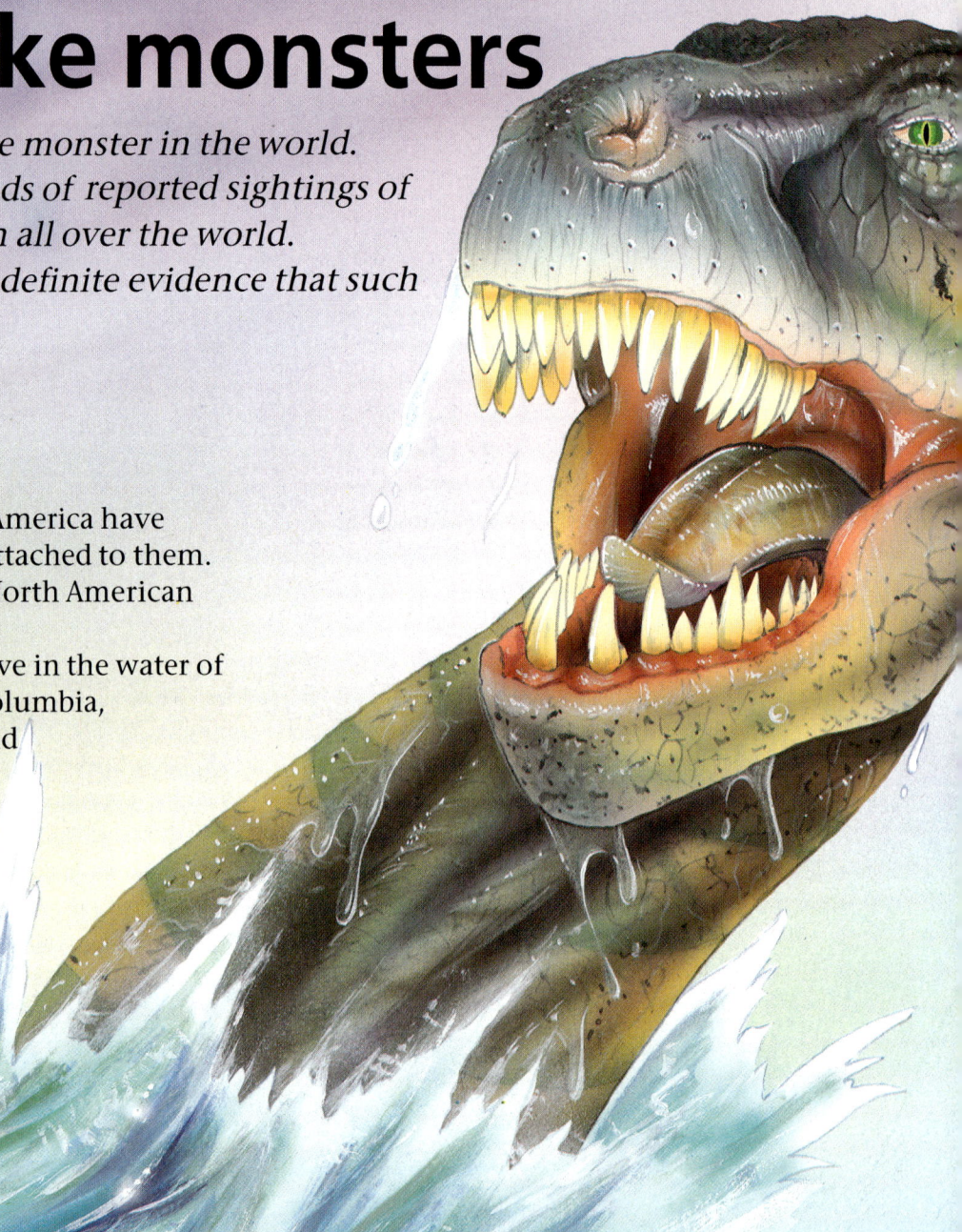

Amazing FACTS

THE NAME OGOPOGO COMES FROM A 1920s BRITISH NONSENSE SONG:

I'M LOOKING FOR THE OGOPOGO, THE FUNNY LITTLE OGOPOGO,
HIS MOTHER WAS AN EARWIG, HIS FATHER WAS A SNAIL,
I'M GOING TO PUT A LITTLE BIT OF SALT ON HIS TAIL,
I WANT TO FIND THE OGOPOGO WHILE HE'S PLAYING HIS OLD BANJO.

The Shushwap Indians used to give offerings to the creature, so as not to offend it. They called it *N'ha-a-itk*, meaning 'Lake Monster' or 'Lake Demon'.

There have been numerous sightings of Ogopogo. These descriptions of the monster are remarkably similar. It is a large, dark-coloured creature, with a long neck and humped back. Like Nessie, photographs and cine film exist of the creature, but they are inconclusive evidence that Ogopogo is really alive.

The Storsjön animal

In Sweden in 1894, a company was formed with the purpose of catching a monster that was supposed to live in Lake Storsjön. This creature, known as the **Storsjön animal**, was described as having short, stumpy feet or legs, big fins, long, webbed hind legs and humps on its back.

A Norwegian whaler was employed to capture the monster. However, despite having a selection of hooks, traps and lines, he failed in his task. After a year of searching, the company went bust. The traps can be seen today in the Östersund museum in Sweden.

Irish lake monsters

Irish legends are full of stories of evil water monsters. They have several names including **piast**, **peiste** and **ullfish**. There are hundreds of remote and mysterious lakes (loughs) in Ireland, and several of these are reputed to be the homes of lake monsters. Most reports of lake monsters come from the counties of Kerry and Galway on the west coast of Ireland.

More world lake monsters

Name	Where sighted
Manipogo	Lake Manitoba, Canada
Slimy Sim	Lake Payette, Idaho, USA
Champ	Lake Champlain, Canada
Ponik	Lake Pohenegamook, Canada
Morag	Loch Morar, Scotland
Waitoreke	Lake Ellesmere, New Zealand

Monsters of the sea

If there are unknown monsters that exist on earth, it is most likely that they live in the sea. Over seventy per cent of the earth is covered in water, much of which remains unexplored. It is not surprising then that there are countless tales of sailors meeting sea serpents and monsters. But like most monster reports, there is no definite evidence to support the existence of these creatures.

The Daedalus sea serpent

On 6 August 1848, the British navy frigate *Daedalus* was sailing in the East Indies when the crew sighted a giant sea serpent.

The Captain, Peter M'quhae, reported the incident when the ship returned home.

The serpent was described as being more than 60 feet (18 metres) long and 2 feet wide. It had the head of a snake and the mane of a horse on its back.

All the crew confirmed this report, even at an official enquiry into the incident.

Would several dozen men all lie or did they really see a sea snake?

Cracking the mystery of the kraken

In the sixteenth century there were several sightings of a sea monster off the coast of Norway. It was named **Kraken**, and was shaped like a giant octopus or squid. According to reports at the time, this monster had several arms and could engulf ships and pull them to the bottom of the sea.

Sailors returning from voyages around the world told stories of multi-armed giant sea monsters. No doubt some of these stories were exaggerated as they were passed from person to person, and experts dismissed the tales.

In 1802, a Frenchman, Denys de Montfort, put forward the view that the Kraken *did* exist. It was not a sea monster, but a giant squid. At first, no one took this seriously, but gradually evidence to support him was gathered.

A 20 metre-long giant squid was caught off the coast of Newfoundland in 1873, and soon after further specimens were caught.

It is now accepted that giant squid *do* exist. They live in deep water, but hunt their food on the surface. Giant squid are the food of some whales and their remains have been discovered in the bellies of whales. It is known also that giant squid and whales fight — perhaps sailing boats were mistaken as whales by the squid and this is why they attacked them.

Underwater people

Every country that has a sea coast has legends of **mermaids** – beautiful women with fish-tails. Mermaids are very careful about their appearance and are often seen combing their hair, but they can also be dangerous. The mermaid's siren song is so magical that it is said to cause sailors to jump overboard and drown.

Mermaids prefer human husbands as **mermen** are very ugly and bad tempered; but if a man ever gives away the secret of his merwife, she goes back to the sea.

Tritons are mermen who live alone in caves beneath the sea. When they are angry, they raise storms. They are often seen as attendants of Neptune, god of the sea.

Selkies are seal people who shed their skins and come ashore as humans. They take a risk when they do this, for they have to leave their skins by the shore. If these skins are found by a human, the selkie cannot return to the sea. If a selkie is hurt, its friends can raise storms and sink ships. They also take revenge on anyone who hurts or kills seals.

Merrows are like mermaids, but must wear red feather caps in order to live under the sea. Male merrows are very ugly but good-natured. Some merrows keep the souls of drowned sailors in cages like pets.

Monster alert!

DON'T PLAY NEAR RIVERS OR PONDS.
IF YOU DO, WATCH OUT FOR:
- *JENNY GREENTEETH*
- *PEG POWLER*
- *NELLY LONGARMS*
- *GRINDY LOW*

THESE ARE ALL WITCHES WHO DRAG NAUGHTY CHILDREN UNDER THE WATER . . .

Mountain monsters

China

Himalayas

Nepal

Bhutan

Bangladesh

Amazing FACTS

IN 1941, A 'HAIRY MAN' WAS CAPTURED IN RUSSIA. THE CREATURE WAS SEEN ALIVE BY A RUSSIAN ARMY COLONEL. IT WAS LATER KILLED AND ITS BODY DISAPPEARED. THERE HAVE BEEN MORE THAN 3,000 REPORTED SIGHTINGS OF THE YOWIE IN AUSTRALIA.

Most people have heard of the **Abominable Snowman** that lives in the Himalayan Mountains. It is also known as a **Yeti**, a Tibetan word that is applied to a real, but unknown animal, or to a mountain spirit or demon.

Many people have claimed to have seen Yetis, but so far nobody has captured one on film.

The only photographic evidence we have for the Yeti's existence are pictures of footprints.

Although the Abominable Snowman is probably the most famous mountain monster, there have been reports of many other 'man beasts' from all around the world. Most of these reports agree about what this 'monster' looks like: it is up to 2.5 metres tall and is covered in reddish-brown hair. It has an ape like face and long arms that reach down to its knees.

These creatures are known by different names in different parts of the world.

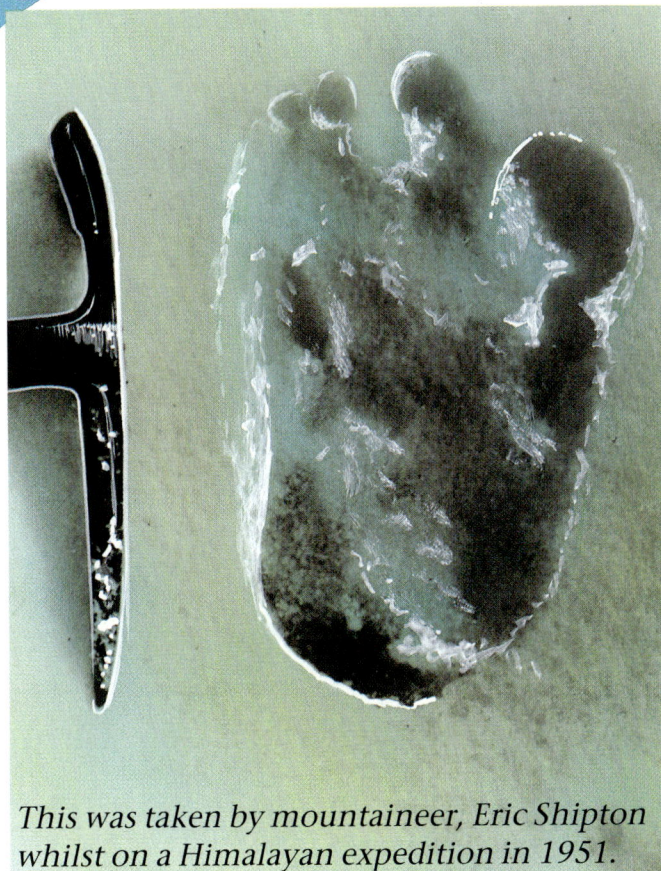

This was taken by mountaineer, Eric Shipton whilst on a Himalayan expedition in 1951.

Place	Name
1 South America (Amazonia)	Maricoxi
2 Africa (Kenya)	Chemosit
3 Australia	Yowie
4 Siberia	Chuchunaa
5 China	Xueren
6 Japan	Hibagon
7 Russia (Caucasus Mountains)	Alma

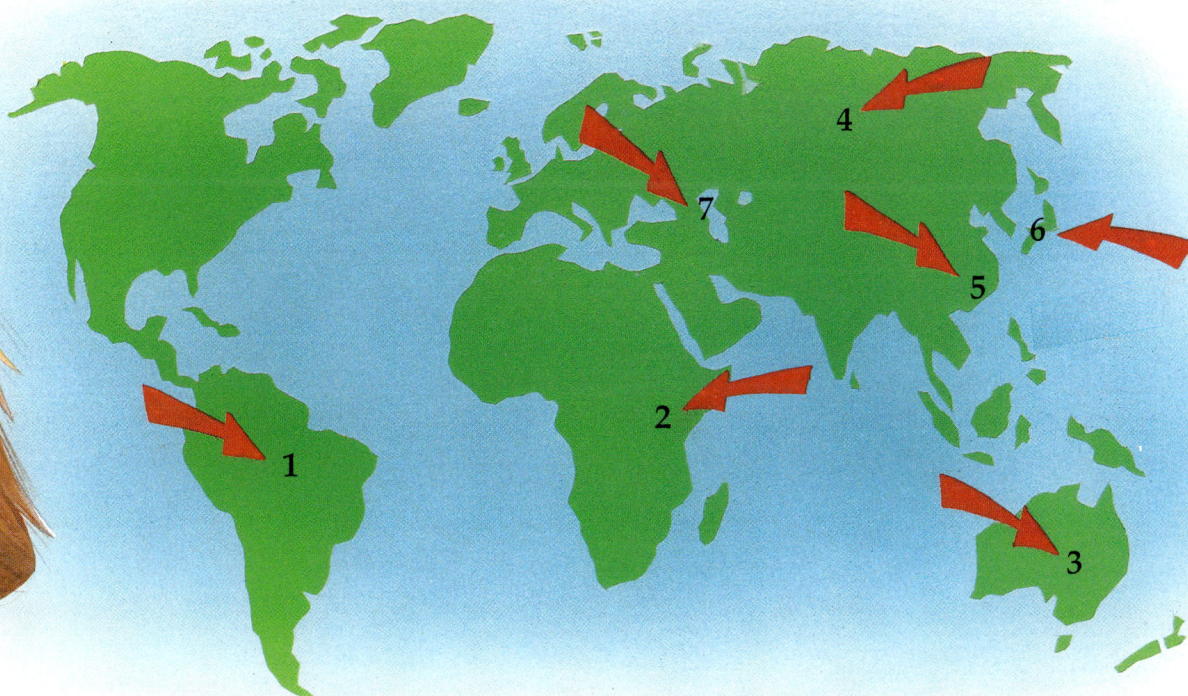

More mountain monsters

The Bigfooted Sasquatch!

Sasquatch is the name given to the mountain monster in North America. Sasquatch is a North American Indian word meaning 'Hairy Giant'.

It is also known as **Bigfoot**, because people have supposedly found footprints of the creature, which have measured over 36 cms. There have been over 1,500 reported sightings of the Sasquatch in the last 150 years. Most of these sightings have occurred in the mountains near the Pacific Ocean.

Canada

British Columbia

West coast of America

USA

This photograph is taken from a cine film shot in 1967 by a Sasquatch hunter called Roger Patterson. He and a friend came across a Sasquatch at Bluff Creek, California. Patterson managed to film the Sasquatch as it moved off.

Many experts have studied the film, and no one has proved it to be fake. In fact, some people claim that this is a female Sasquatch carrying a baby Sasquatch.

Some experts say that it isn't Bigfoot at all but a person dressed in animal skins.

Strange...
but is it true?

In 1924, Albert Ostman, a gold prospector in British Columbia, Canada, claimed that he was kidnapped by a Sasquatch and taken home to its family! Ostman said that he was kept captive for several days before he managed to escape by giving the 'old man' some snuff (powdered tobacco). The Sasquatch sniffed this and had to rush out to get some water. Ostman took his chance and fled for his life.

Scientists in China have discovered the fossils of a giant ape, GIGANTOPITHECUS. By examining the fossils, the scientists have calculated that this type of ape lived between 12 million and 500,000 years ago. Some people say that the present day manbeasts are descended from this ape.

Real monsters?

Some monsters have been the result of people mixing up fact and fantasy. Descriptions of real creatures have been exaggerated and changed as they were retold.

Could they have been . . .

The unicorn

Stories of the Unicorn have been handed down for thousands of years. This mythical creature was supposed to be a beautiful white horse-like creature, with a single horn on its forehead. This horn was supposed to have magical properties when made into a powder and taken by humans.

The rhinoceros

It was Ctesias, an ancient Greek writer, who first mentioned the unicorn. He was writing about the animals of India. He claimed that the unicorn was as large as a horse, had a white body, a red head and a horn on its snout. The writer was almost certainly describing a rhinoceros! The rhinoceros is the only one-horned animal in the world. Could it be the mythical unicorn?

The unicorn whale

The Narwhal is a whale that has a spiral tusk. These tusks can grow up to three metres long. In medieval times the tusk of the Narwhal was often sold as a unicorn's horn.

In many paintings of the time, the unicorn is shown as having a spiral tusk, like the Narwhals.

Mermaids and mermen

From ancient times, sailors have told stories of seeing mermaids and mermen stretched out on rocks and shorelines.

Seals

Many species of seals rest on rocks and shorelines. Some of these can appear human-like when seen from a distance. It is quite probable than many sailors mistook these for mermaids.

Cryptozoology

Despite the fact that some monsters can be explained as being the product of real creatures combined with over imagination, people take the subject of monster hunting very seriously. They believe that there are unknown creatures waiting to be discovered. The study of animals that may or may not exist is called **cryptozoology**.

People who believe that the Loch Ness Monster could be a plesiosaur are not put off by the fact that the plesiosaur is a prehistoric creature believed to have been extinct for 70 million years! Cryptozoologists point out that a fish called the coelacanth, thought to have died out millions of years ago, was found in the Indian Oceans in 1938. Since then several others have been caught.

Amazing FACTS

THE OKAPI IS ANOTHER ANIMAL THAT GIVES SUPPORT TO CRYPTOZOOLOGISTS' ARGUMENTS THAT THERE ARE ANIMALS WAITING TO BE DISCOVERED.
THE OKAPI IS A REAL ANIMAL, BEING A CROSS BETWEEN A ZEBRA AND A GIRAFFE. DESPITE

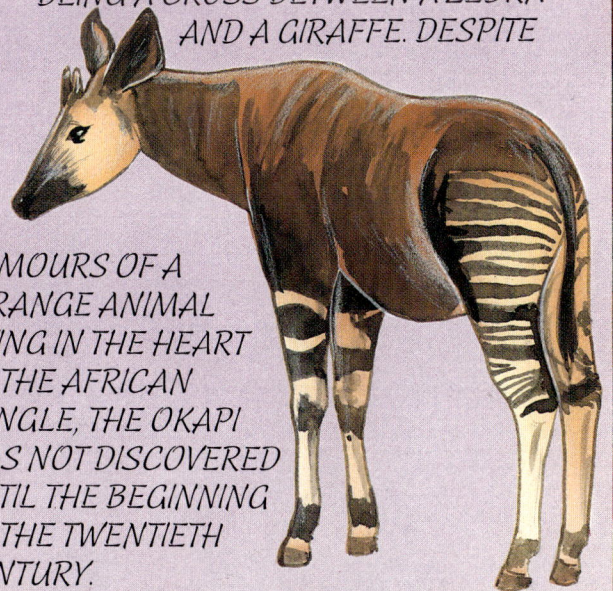

RUMOURS OF A STRANGE ANIMAL LIVING IN THE HEART OF THE AFRICAN JUNGLE, THE OKAPI WAS NOT DISCOVERED UNTIL THE BEGINNING OF THE TWENTIETH CENTURY.

Mythical monsters of Ancient Greece and Rome

The myths and legends of the ancient world are full of monsters. Were these all simply in the imagination of storytellers, or did they once exist upon Earth?

The Gorgon Medusa

The Gorgon's very glance could turn anyone who met her into stone. The hero Perseus, wearing a helmet of invisibility, killed her by looking at her reflection in his shield as he cut her head off with his sword.

The Hydra

The breath of the Hydra was so foul that it could kill. The Greek hero, Heracles, fought the monster, but discovered that every time he crushed one of its heads, two or three more grew in its place.

The Griffin

One of the fiercest and most impressive of mythological creatures, the Griffin is a favourite creature in Heraldry.

Centaurs

Centaurs are usually thought of nowadays as being half human, half horse, and have a reputation for wisdom and skill in archery; but in the original Greek myths they are more goat-like.

The Minotaur

Asterion, the Minotaur, lived in the labyrinth beneath the palace of Minos in Crete, devouring human sacrifices. He was killed by Theseus.

Basilisk (or Cockatrice)

The Basilisk was one of the smallest of the mythical monsters, and also one of the deadliest. It was hatched by a lizard from a cock's egg. Since cocks do not lay many eggs, the Basilisk was rare. One look from it was enough to kill a person. Only three things could kill a Basilisk: a weasel, a cock crowing or the sight of its own reflection in a mirror.

More mythical monsters!

In Hindu mythology, **Mahisha** was an enormous demon water buffalo. His power was so great that he had taken control over the world.

Not even the great gods Vishnu or Shiva could face up to the monster. In order to defeat Mahisha, the gods joined together to create the goddess Devi.

Taking the form of Durga, a ten-armed fighter, Devi rode into battle on a tiger.

She managed to strike the buffalo with her weapon, whereupon the demon changed into a thousand-armed giant with a thousand weapons.

Durga grabbed Mahisha by the arms and threw him to the ground. She killed the demon monster by stabbing him with an arrow.

Gigantic trouble!

There are many stories of giants in the mythology of North America.

Dzoavatis appears in the stories of the Shoshonean Indians who live in the American states of Utah, Idaho and Nevada.

Dzoavatis was an ugly ogre who stole the children of Dove. But thanks to the help of the animals, Crane, Eagle and Badger, the children escaped and Dzoavatis was blocked up in a hole in the ground.

Beowulf is the oldest surviving epic poem in English. It tells the story of Beowulf and his struggles with the giant monsters Grendel and his mother. Grendel was a mighty monster who lived in the marshes of Denmark. He killed many of King Hrothgar's men before the hero Beowulf killed him. Grendel's mother sought revenge, but she too suffered the same fate at the hands of Beowulf, 'the Dragon Slayer'.

Dragons!

The dragon is one of the oldest mythological monsters. It features in stories from all over the world and appears in many different forms.

Dragons of the West

In the Western world and Africa, dragons are thought of as evil creatures. They are usually dangerous, fire breathing reptiles, that go around destroying land, killing people and demanding human sacrifices.

They are associated with demons and devils and are often the target for heroes to prove themselves by killing a dragon. The most famous dragon killer in western mythology is St George. He saved the citizens of Sylene from a dragon that was terrorising the city. In return for killing the dragon, he demanded that the people of Sylene should become Christians. There were different types of western dragons:

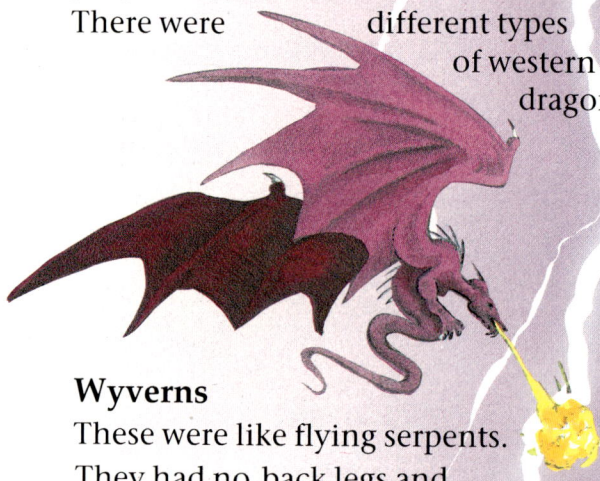

According to legend, a huge dragon lies at the roots of the earth with its tail grasped in its teeth. It is called the worm ouroboros by some, and the midgarth serpent or jormungand by others.

Wyverns

These were like flying serpents. They had no back legs and rested on their tails and front legs.

Boas

These were snake-like creatures who were accused of sucking herds of cattle dry before eating them.

Firedrakes

These were miniature fire-breathing dragons. They tended to guard great hoards of treasure and lived in deep caves.

Dragons of the East

In Chinese mythology, dragons (known as *lung*) were thought of as being kindly and benevolent. They were associated with the gods and became the symbol of power for many Chinese emperors. There were many festivals and celebrations in honour of dragons and even today, the dragon holds a special place in Chinese New Year celebrations.

Below are the different types of Chinese dragons:

Ti Lung

This dragon was the controller of all rivers and streams.

Tiens Lung

This dragon supported the mansions of the gods.

Shen Lung

This dragon was the bringer of rain.

Fu-Ts'ang Lung

This dragon was the keeper of hidden treasure and of all the precious metals in the earth.

Amazing FACTS

THE WORD 'DRAGON' COMES FROM THE ANCIENT GREEK WORD DRAKON MEANING 'SHARP SIGHTED ONE'. THIS LATER CAME TO MEAN 'GIANT SNAKE'.

IN MEDIEVAL TIMES, DRAGONS AND SERPENTS WERE CALLED 'WORMS'.

Transformation monsters!

Some monsters are shape-changers: they are human in one form, but can change into hideous creatures.

Werewolves

A werewolf is a human being that changes into a wolf by the light of the full moon. If victims of a werewolf bite do not die, they become werewolves themselves. Werewolves cannot be killed by ordinary means, they must be shot with silver bullets.

Did you Know?

IT IS THOUGHT THAT WEREWOLF STORIES CAME ABOUT THROUGH EXAGGERATED STORIES OF THE EFFECTS OF RABIES.

PEOPLE WHO BEHAVE LIKE WOLVES ARE SUFFERING FROM A DISEASE KNOWN AS LYCANTHROPY.

Dracula

Perhaps the most famous horror monster of all time is Dracula, a vampire. He lives by drinking blood. Dracula has the power to turn himself into a bat to seek fresh victims.

Vampire bashing!

How to keep vampires away:
- Eat a lot or garlic and spread it all round your room. (This will keep everyone else away, too.)
- Making the sign of a cross is also bad news for vampires.

How to spot a vampire:
- Vampires have no reflection in a mirror.

How to destroy a vampire:
- Like a werewolf, a vampire can be killed with a silver bullet.
- A more sure-fire method is to drive a stake through the vampire's heart.
- Vampires sleep during the day and can be destroyed by exposure to sunlight.

Amazing FACTS

THE ORIGINAL DRACULA IS THOUGHT TO HAVE BEEN A CRUEL LORD CALLED VLAD THE IMPALER, AS IT WAS HIS HABIT TO HAVE SPIKES DRIVEN THROUGH THE BODIES OF THOSE WHO DISPLEASED HIM.

Monster-spotting

You walk past hundreds of monsters every day!
They look down at you from walls, flagpoles, hillsides and buses!
They can even be looking up at you from the packaging on food!

Do you recognise these monsters?

1

2

Yummy!

3

4

5

6

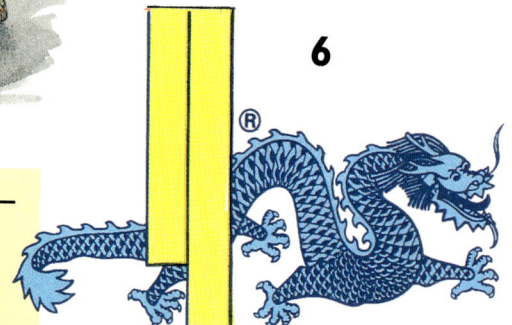

Look around and see what other monsters you can spot!

24

Heraldry

You will spot many monsters on coats of arms. In the middle ages, knights wore armour to protect themselves in battle. This meant that their faces could not be seen and people didn't know who was inside the armour! In order to stop this confusion and help to identify who they were, each knight had a coat of arms which he wore, painted on his shield.

This idea caught on and soon countries, cities, towns, schools and colleges and even churches had their own coats of arms.

The study of these is called **heraldry**.

Did you Know?

THERE ARE SPECIAL RULES CONCERNING WHAT COATS OF ARMS CAN LOOK LIKE. THE RULES ARE HUNDREDS OF YEARS OLD AND ARE STILL USED TODAY.

Crest — Mantling

Torse

Helm

Supporter — Supporter

The Arms on a Shield

CUSTODI DOMINE CIVITATEM

Motto — Compartment

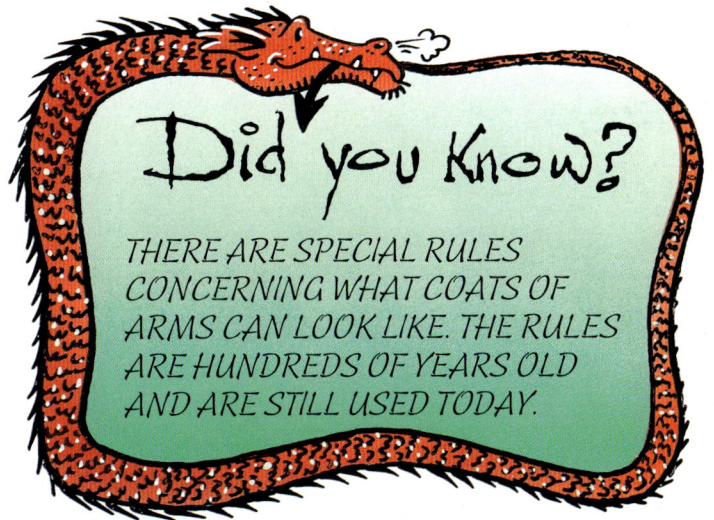

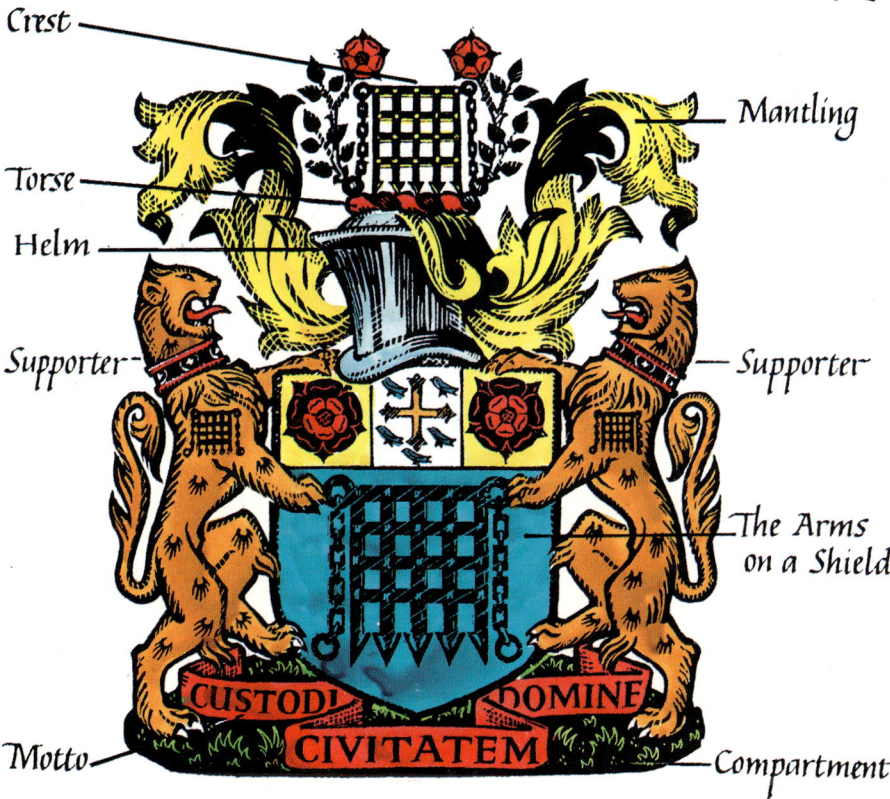

The most popular monsters in heraldry are dragons, unicorns, griffins and wyverns.

Stone Monsters

On many churches and castles you will find **gargoyles**. These are imps and demons with grotesque faces. Sometimes their mouths are waterspouts. They are supposed to keep evil spirits away.

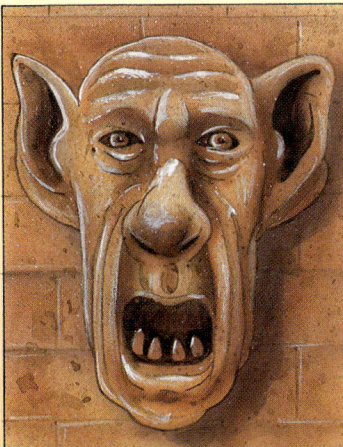

25

Man-made monsters

Frankenstein's creature

In Mary Shelley's novel, *Frankenstein*, Victor Frankenstein tries to create a superhuman creature by using electricity to reanimate a body made up of 'spare parts' of corpses. Not surprisingly, the hideous result of his experiment frightens Frankenstein into fits. Feeling alone and rejected, the creature he has made turns into an evil monster.

Robots and androids

Robots first appeared in a play by Karel Capek called *R.U.R.*, 'Rossum's Universal Robots' (1921), in which artificial humans revolt against the people who exploit them.

Probably the most famous robots are R2D2 and C3P0 from the *Star Wars* films.

A Robot can be any shape, but robots that look like people are often called **Androids**.

Isaac Asimov wrote many books about 'positronic robots'. These robots are designed to help humans, and are programmed with the Three Laws of Robotics but sometimes they go out of control.

The most villainous of all robots, however, is a computer, **Hal 9000**, who controls the spaceship *Discovery* in the novel and film *2001: A Space Odyssey*. Hal tries to murder all the humans on the ship rather than have to admit that 'he' has made a mistake . . .

Did you know?

ROBOT IS A CZECH WORD MEANING WORKER.
ROBOTS IN SOUTHERN AFRICA ARE TRAFFIC LIGHTS!

Isaac Asimov's Three Laws of Robotics:

1 A robot may not injure a human being, or, through inaction, allow a human being to come to harm.
2 A robot must obey the orders given to it by human beings except where such orders would conflict with the First Law.
3 A robot must protect its own existence as long as such protection does not conflict with the First or Second Law.

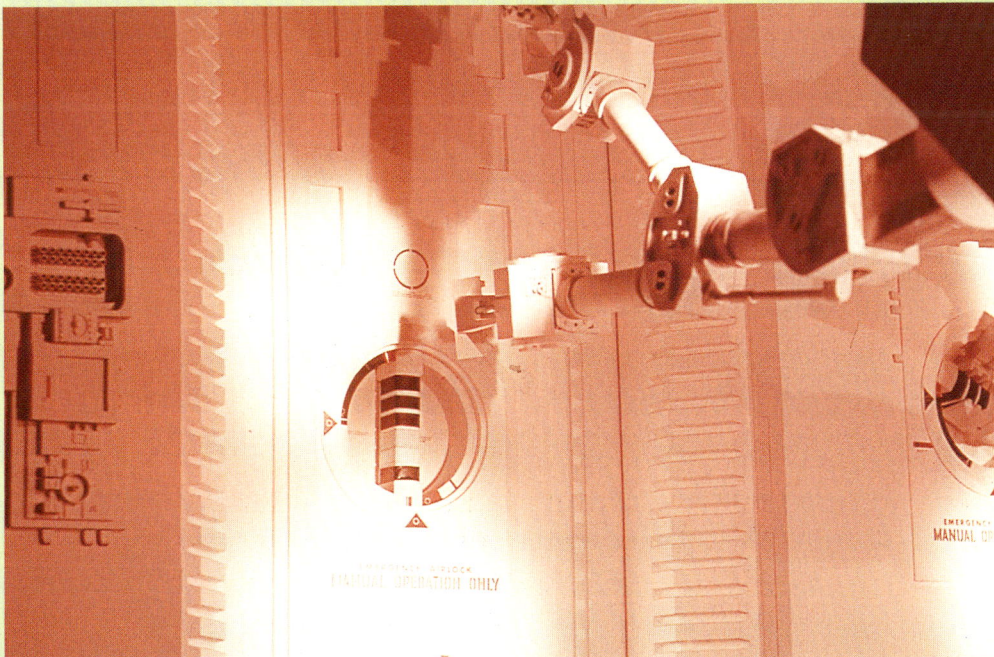

Science fiction and fantasy monsters

Many people create monsters. They do this to frighten and entertain us. The monsters on these pages have all been created by people's imaginations.

Triffids

In John Wyndham's book, *The Day of the Triffids,* most of the population of the earth is blinded in a freak accident. Walking plants, over two metres tall, with whiplike stings containing poison powerful enough to kill a human being, take over the world!

Martians

For years, science fiction writers have speculated about what creatures might live on Mars.

In H G Wells' book, *The War of the Worlds*, the martians invade the earth in spaceships and build giant three-legged robots armed with heat-rays to conquer the world. People's weapons prove useless, but the martians are eventually destroyed by common germs, against which they have no defence.

King Kong

A group of explorers discover a mysterious island inhabited by dinosaurs and monsters, whose lord is a giant ape, known to the islanders as 'King Kong'. Kong is eventually captured and taken back to New York as a curiosity – but the creature escapes.

Did you know?

THERE ARE SO MANY MONSTERS IN SCIENCE FICTION AND FANTASY BOOKS, THAT THEY HAVE A SPECIAL NAME. THEY ARE CALLED BEMS, WHICH IS SHORT FOR BUG EYED MONSTERS.

A monster map

There are stories of monsters from all around the world. Most of these monsters are from legends and myths. Some of them may really exist.

In Scandinavian mythology, the word **Troll** describes any kind of monster. Nowadays, a Troll is thought of as a type of elf or fairy.

A **Quiqion** is an enormous hairless dog, feared by the Eskimos. When people approach it, they suffer fits. However, it is easily frightened and can be scared off by shouting its name.

A **Squonk** is a shy beast that lives in the forests of Pennsylvania. It is so ugly that it cries out of self-pity. If it is captured, the Squonk dissolves itself, leaving behind only tears and bubbles.

An **Ihuaivulu** is a seven-headed fire monster, believed by South American Indians to have caused volcanoes to erupt.

A **Were-Jaguar** is the equivalent of a Werewolf. Like a werewolf, it is a human transformed into an animal form. Were-Jaguars exist in South American legends and stories.

Mngwa means 'the strange one'. It is the most feared and mysterious monster in central Africa. It has a cat-like appearance and rips up anybody who meets it.

The **Naga** is a god-like creature, with a human head and a serpent's body. Nagas live in underground palaces, or the depths of the Earth.

The **Kappa** is a Japanese river goblin. It has a body of a tortoise, the face of an ape and scaly arms and legs. The Kappa eats humans and the only way to overpower it is to be polite to it!

The **Nasnas** is a legendary creature from the Middle East. The Nasnas has human features, except it only has one leg, one arm and half a face and body.

The **Chinese Wildman** version of the Yeti and the Sasquatch. The wildman is supposed to live in forests in the Hubei Province in central China. There have been many reported sightings of the creature.

The **Hai Ho Shang** is a monster fish with a shaved head. These legendary monsters lived in the South China Seas, capsizing ships and causing their crews to drown.

The **Manticore** is an Indian creature, with a man's head, a lion's body and a scorpion's tail that fires arrows.

The **Nandi bear** is also called **Chemosit**. It is a giant flesh-eating bear from Kenya. It is supposed to eat the brains of its victims.

The **Waitoreke** is a huge otter-like water monster.
   The Waitoreke is thought to live in the deep lakes of South Island, New Zealand.

Index

Abominable Snowman	11	Hai Ho Shang	31	Okapi	15
Alma	11	Hal 9000	27	Ogopogo	4
Androids	27	Hibagon	11	Peg Powler	9
Basilisk	16	Hydra	17	Piast	5
BEMs	29	Ihuaivulu	30	Ponik	5
Bigfoot	12	Jenny Greenteeth	9	Quiqion	30
Boas	20	Jormungand	21	Rhinoceros	14
Centaurs	17	Kappa	31	Robots	27
Champ	5	King Kong	29	Sasquatch	12–13
Chemosit	11	Kraken	7	Sea Serpent	6
Chinese Wildman	31	Lung (Tien, Shen Ti,		Selkies	9
Chuchunaa	11	Fu T'sang)	21	Slimy Sim	5
Cockatrice	16	Mahisha	18	Squonk	30
Coeclacanth	15	Manipono	5	Storsjön Animal	5
Dracula	23	Manticore	31	Triffids	28
Dragons	20 – 21	Maricoxi	11	Triton	8
Durgu	18	Martians	29	Trolls	30
Dzouvatis	19	Medusa	16	Ullfish	5
Firedrakes	20	Mermaids	8, 15	Unicorn	14
Frankenstein's creature	26	Mermen	8, 15	Vampires	23
Gargoyles	24	Merrows	9	Waitoreke	5, 31
Gigantopithecus	13	Midgarth Serpent	21	Were-jaguar	30
Gorgon	16	Minotaur	17	Werewolf	22
Grendel	19	Mngwa	30	World Serpent	21
Griffin	17	Morag	5	Worm Ouroboros	21
Grindy Low	9	Nandi Bear	31	Wyvern	21
		Naga	31	Xueren	11
		Narwhal	14	Yeti	10
		Nasnas	31	Yowie	11
		Nelly Longarms	9		
		Nessie	2-3		

British Library Cataloguing in Publication Data

Barlow, Steve
  Monsters Project Book
  I. Title II. Skidmore, Steve
  001.9

  ISBN 1-86019-541-5

First published 1993

© 1993 Steve Barlow and Steve Skidmore

This edition published 1997 by Brockhampton Press, a member of Hodder Headline PLC Group.
10 9 8 7 6 5 4 3 2 1
1999 1998 1997

Typeset by Litho Link Ltd, Welshpool, Powys, Wales.
Printed in India.

Acknowledgements

The author and publishers would like to thank the following for permission to reproduce photographic material in this book:

Academy of Applied Science p. 3; British Film Institute p. 22; British Film Institute/Movie Acquisition Corporation Ltd. p. 23; British Film Institute/MCA p. 26; British Film Institute/Lucas Film Ltd. p. 27; British Film Institute/Turner Entertainment Corporation p. 27; British Film Institute p. 28; British Film Institute/Paramount Picture Corporation p. 29; British Film Institute/Turner Entertainment Corporation p.29; Fortean Picture Library p. 2, 6, 13; National History Museum p. 7; Royal Geographical Society p. 11. Product images on p.24 courtesy of the following: Blue Dragon,© St Ivel; Midland Bank Ltd; Monster Munch words and characters are a registered trade mark of Smiths Crisps Ltd; Sugar Puffs, a trade mark of Quaker Oats Ltd.